## DATE DUE

| Mar. 18 | | | |
|---|---|---|---|
| MAY 2 4 1966 | | | |
| MAR 12 '68 | | | |
| MAR 26 '68 | | | |
| MAR 28 68 | | | |
| APR 1 8 1968 | | | |
| JAN 2 3 1990 | | | |
| JAN 1 6 1990 | | | |
| | | | |
| | | | |
| | | | |
| | | | |
| | | | |
| | | | |
| | | | |
| | | | |
| GAYLORD | | | PRINTED IN U.S.A. |

# The FIRST BOOK of
# SWITZERLAND

# The FIRST BOOK of
# SWITZERLAND

*by Sam and Beryl Epstein*
*Illustrated with photographs*

FRANKLIN WATTS, INC.
575 Lexington Avenue • New York 22

Library of Congress Catalog Card Number: 64-11911
Copyright © 1964 by Franklin Watts, Inc.
Printed in the United States of America
by Polygraphic Company of America, Inc.

1   2   3   4   5   6   7

# Contents

# The FIRST BOOK of
# SWITZERLAND

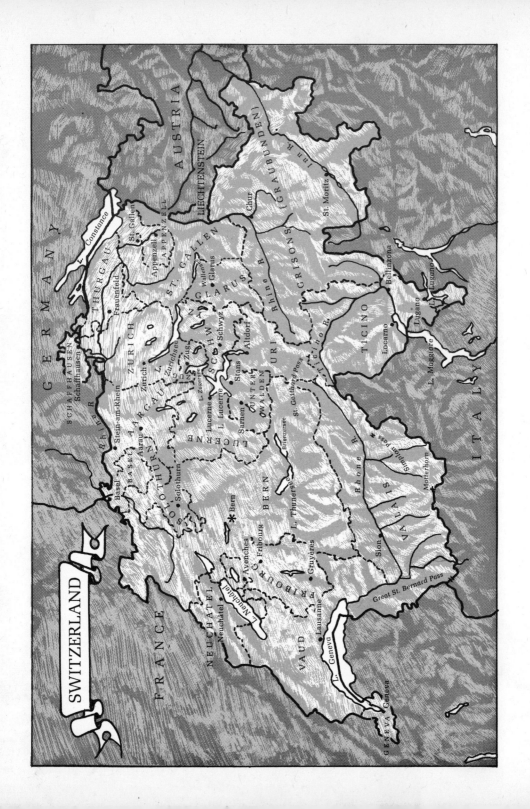

# Mountains, Mountains Everywhere

ALMOST EVERYBODY in Switzerland lives on the side of a mountain, at the foot of a mountain, or within sight of a mountain. Mountains are the background for almost everything that happens in this tiny republic at the heart of Europe. They are the reason for most of the happenings, too.

Because rushing mountain streams can produce a great deal of electricity, Swiss factories and trains operate electrically, and even the smallest Swiss village has electric light.

Because Switzerland's snow-capped Alps attract millions of visitors every year, the country has more hotels and inns and restaurants than many places twice its size.

Because Switzerland's mountains contain no great amount of iron or other minerals, many of the raw materials used in Swiss factories must be imported.

Because the mountains leave Switzerland with very little fertile soil, she can grow only about three-fifths of the food her population needs, and must import some foodstuffs.

*Switzerland is less than twice the size of New Jersey, but if its peaks and ridges could be flattened out, it would cover an area almost as large as Texas*

*A 930-foot-high dam — the world's highest when it was finished in 1961 — helps provide electric power*

The Swiss are among the most prosperous people in all Europe. They have achieved their high standard of living partly because of their mountains, but mostly in spite of them. They have won their prosperity largely because they have learned special skills and abilities that people who live in flatter, richer, and more fertile lands do not need.

Swiss engineers, for example, have learned how to lay roads and railroad tracks that corkscrew up and down steep grades, tunnel through solid rock more than a mile underground, and cross chasms on high bridges. One of these bridges is built so that it can be folded safely back against a cliff during the winter avalanche season.

Swiss craftsmen have learned how to transform expensive imported raw materials into products of such high quality that they

2

*. . . for Swiss railways, factories, towns, and villages*

can be sold at a profit in the world's markets. That profit not only pays for the materials themselves, but also gives Switzerland a money balance to spend on food imported from other countries.

Swiss fruit- and vinegrowers have learned how to train a fruit tree or a grapevine against a wall or on wires so that it occupies very little space.

Swiss cattle and sheep farmers have learned how to take advantage of every patch of green pasture by moving their herds uphill and downhill with the seasons.

All of these special skills and abilities — some new, some very old — grow out of the need for 5 ½ million people to make a living in one of the most mountainous countries in the world.

3

*Setting out for the mountain pastures*

# Uphill and Downhill

IN MANY SWISS villages the word *inalpe* is used for the spring day when cattle are led out of their dark winter stables and driven uphill to fresh green Alpine pastures. In these villages, life still follows a pattern that is many centuries old.

*Inalpe* takes place late in May or early in June, as soon as the snow has melted on the pastures that are several thousand feet higher than the village itself. *Inalpe* is always a day of great excitement.

In a village of the Valais, for example — the Valais is a region in southwestern Switzerland — the excitement begins at dawn. The

4

*The path is steep and dangerous*

school term has ended for the season. Children are everywhere. Dogs bark. Chickens cackle. Mules complain noisily when they are loaded with heavy baskets of food, rolls of blankets, and other supplies. Suddenly the narrow streets between the close-packed houses are crowded with cattle, restless after long months indoors. The big bells around their necks jangle loudly.

At last everything is ready. The man chosen as the chief shepherd leads a long, straggling procession out of the village and up the forested slope rising behind it. Other men, assisted by boys and dogs, drive the cattle behind him. The animals are surefooted, but the path is steep and dangerous, often skirting the edge of a cliff. Everyone is on the alert every moment, to make sure that no creature slips and falls to its death. After the cattle come most of the women and children of the village, and the laden mules.

SWISS NATIONAL TOURIST OFFICE

*Melting cheese for the dish called* raclette

The journey lasts about three hours, and ends in a big, stone-walled meadow. Before the last cows arrive, the first are already feasting hungrily on the new grass sprinkled with blue gentian flowers.

The men inspect the stone stables at one end of the meadow, to make sure they have survived the winter's weight of snow. The women examine the small wooden houses, or chalets, that stand near the stables. They open the doors and fling back the heavy wooden shutters, to let in the spring sunlight.

Each chalet holds a table and benches, rough bunks for beds, and a big kettle hanging on a crane in the stone fireplace. There are a few pans and dishes on a shelf. The little house is not nearly as comfortable as the village home each woman has left behind, but it is snug and clean.

Soon the older boys are building a fire in the open. One by one, the villagers gather around it, ready for the picnic meal that will celebrate their arrival.

They eat *raclette*, a popular Valais dish made from the local cheese, which is also called *raclette*. A thick, round wheel of the cheese, more than a foot across, is cut in half. One of the men holds the cut side close to the fire. As soon as the cheese begins to melt, he scrapes the softened layer off onto a plate. It is eaten with bread or boiled potatoes, and juicy pickles.

Everybody is hungry after the long, uphill climb. Most people have several helpings of *raclette*.

After dinner the cattle must be watered at big troughs carved out of tree trunks. Then it is milking time.

By sundown the children are tired out after the excitement of the day. Their mothers put them to bed in the little mountain chalets where the village families will spend the next several weeks.

*The watering trough*

At the end of that time, in late June or early July, the grass will be green in pastures still higher in the Alps, right at the foot of perpetually frozen glaciers. Then the cattle will be moved uphill again, to those fields.

Only the men and boys who are the official village shepherds will accompany the herd on that journey. At its end they will find more small wooden chalets, crudely furnished, which will be their homes until autumn. They will spend most of their time out of doors, milking the cattle morning and evening, and making the big rounds of *raclette* cheese that they will take home in September.

In the meantime the women, the smaller children, and the rest of the men who made the journey to the first uphill pasture have returned to their village. There, with the few who stayed behind on the day of *inalpe*, they take up their summer work.

The men may be mountain guides or foresters, bakers or shopkeepers. One family may run an inn. Women and children tend the pigs and chickens and bees that many families keep, and cultivate the small fields and gardens that were planted earlier in the year.

The growing season is short here. Farmers scatter black soil on the snow in the spring, to hasten its melting so that seeds can be sown.

Every inch of fertile soil is used. Vines grow on terraces hacked out of a hillside. A few vegetable plants are tucked into each tiny pocket of soil between outcropping rocks. Hay grows in all the larger open areas.

The hay is cut the moment it is ripe. If a storm threatens, everyone in the village works from dawn until after dark to get the crop under shelter before it is ruined. Then, on wooden platforms inside the stables, the villagers toss the hay with big forks so that it will dry evenly all through.

*Families join their cattle at the mountain pasture for a few weeks each summer*

The hay crop is never very big, but it is valuable. It will feed the cattle during the long, cold months ahead. If the crop fails, or spoils because it is not properly dried, fodder must be bought at the nearest town. Then the village families must do without most of the other things they usually buy with their small cash incomes. They never go hungry, but they live closer to the edge of poverty than most of the Swiss do.

The day of *exalpe* is a holiday, too—the day when the shepherds bring the herd back from the high summer fields. Usually the rest of the villagers walk as far as the first hill pasture to meet the home-comers and accompany them on the last stage of their journey.

When the cattle are all safely back at the village, they are driven into stone-walled pens. There each owner picks out his animals, and counts the new calves that have been born to his cows during the summer.

Then the cheeses made during the summer are weighed and distributed. The amount of cheese each cattle owner receives is in proportion to the amount of milk his animals gave during the season. Usually he puts several cheeses away for his own family's use, and sells the rest in the nearest big town.

ELISABETH THEILER-BUCHI

*This Swiss embroidery tells the story of* inalpe

*Every farmer stores a few cheeses for his own family*

By the time the first snow falls on the village, the cattle are stabled and the crops are harvested and stored.

The village school opens again. The mountain children must cram a whole year of study into their short winter term. They work hard at their lessons six days a week.

The women take up the embroidery and lacemaking that they put away the previous May.

The men tend their cattle and other livestock, and do any other work that comes to hand. A few still carve the same kind of elaborate wooden chests and chairs their grandfathers made. Those who spent the summer as mountain guides are now giving ski instructions at the big resort hotel not far away.

All the men use their time as thriftily as they use their land. Along with their wives and their sons and daughters, they keep busy all during the long Alpine winter until the day of *inalpe*, the following spring.

11

*The ancient village of Gruyères stands high on a hill above a rich valley*

# Swiss Cheese – and Chocolate

MILK is the one food product Switzerland produces in a quantity greater than she needs. It is excellent milk, creamy and rich. It makes good butter, cheese, and chocolate candy. Switzerland exports all these products in exchange for some of the grains and other foods she cannot grow herself.

Most of the cheese she exports is the kind Americans call Swiss — the cheese with holes in it. This may be either one of two similar cheeses that the Swiss themselves call Emmentaler and Gruyère. Each is named for the region in Switzerland where it is made.

A cheese-making factory in the Emmental is an up-to-date dairy run according to strict government regulations. Usually it is owned by a group of farmers, perhaps several dozens of them. They have built the dairy at a central place convenient to all their farms. They rent it to a professional cheese maker who agrees to buy the entire production of their herds.

12

Every morning and every evening, when a farmer finishes milking his cows, he pours the fresh, warm milk into big cans, each holding about fifty quarts. He loads the cans on a truck, or a small cart drawn by a dog or a pony, and sends them to the dairy. Usually one of his younger sons is responsible for taking the milk to the dairy twice a day. Or a man may take his milk to the dairy in a flat can that can be strapped to his back.

*Milk arrives at the cheese factory twice a day, morning and evening*

*Pouring the milk into the vats*

The cheese maker and his assistants pour the fresh milk into big copper vats. Then each vat, which may hold as much as 1,200 quarts, is warmed to a temperature of about 95 degrees. It is kept warm until the milk ferments, and in so doing forms a substance called lactic acid.

When the milk contains just the right amount of acid, the cheese maker adds a substance called rennet, and stirs it in thoroughly. Soon the milk begins to curdle — to separate into a curd and a whey. The whey is a thin, watery liquid. The curd is the thick, white, jelly-like mass from which the cheese will be made.

Some of the whey collects quickly on top of the curd. The rest remains trapped inside the jelly-like mass. To get rid of that whey, the cheese maker cuts the curd into small pieces, using wooden shovels and an instrument strung with wires, which looks rather like a harp. The wires slice through the curd, letting the whey drain out and float to the surface. Usually the whey is skimmed off and returned to the farmers, who feed it to their hogs.

14

*Cutting cheese curds with wooden shovels*

*. . . then with an instrument strung with wires*

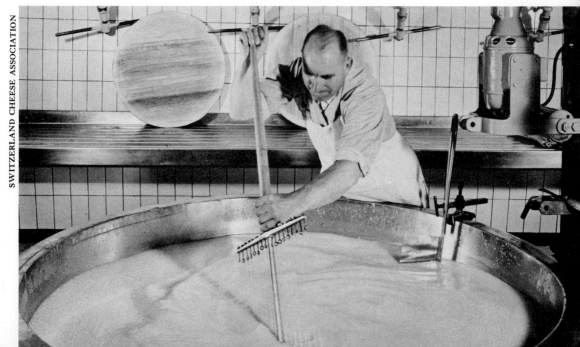

SWITZERLAND CHEESE ASSOCIATION

*Removing the curd from the vat*

The curd left in the vat is then heated again, and stirred steadily for hours. A mechanical stirring device can be used for this process.

After sufficient stirring, it is time to remove the curd from the vat. The cheese maker scoops it up with a device rather like a big butterfly net — a cloth fastened to a frame. Then he removes the frame, and ties the corners of the cloth together to form a bag. Using a tackle and an overhead rail, he lifts the heavy, dripping bag out of the vat and sets it in a round wooden mold on a table. The mold is almost a yard across and almost a foot high.

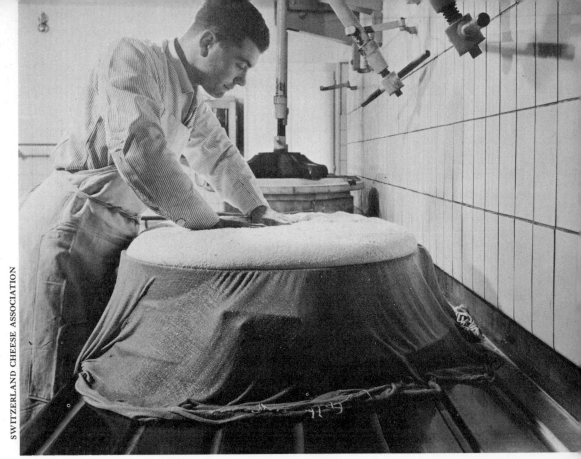

*Filling the wooden cheese mold*

After the curd has been firmly pressed into the mold, it is left there for twenty-four hours. During that period it is turned over several times, and the mold is tightened in order to squeeze out the last of the whey.

The dry curd is next removed from its mold, and floated in salt water for several days. Finally, after being stored in a cool cellar for a brief time, the big wheel of cheese is moved to a shelf in a warm cellar, where it is left until it is ripe.

The ripening process takes place slowly, and lasts for two or three

*Ripening cheese demands constant attention*

months. During that time, bubbles of gas form inside the cheese. Those bubbles make the eyes, or holes, for which Swiss cheese is famous.

Ripening cheese demands constant attention. Every two days each big wheel must be taken from its shelf, turned over, rubbed with a dry cloth, sprinkled with salt, and put back on its shelf again.

Gradually a yellowish-brown rind forms on the outside of the wheel of cheese. The interior is changing color, too. Cheese made from winter milk, produced while the cows are being fed dry hay,

18

becomes a very pale cream color. Cheese made from the summer milk of pasture-fed cows turns a deeper shade of cream.

When the cheese maker thinks a cheese is almost ripe, he taps it. He knows just how a cheese should sound under his tapping finger, if its eyes have reached the right size — if the ripening process has gone on long enough. The eyes of a ripe Emmentaler are about the size of a cherry, or a little larger, and the cheese has a delicate, nutty flavor.

The moment a cheese is fully ripe, it is moved to a cool place so that the eyes will not grow any larger. There it is stored until a cheese dealer makes his regular visit to the dairy and takes it away.

Gruyère cheese is made by much the same method as Emmentaler, but in smaller wheels. It has smaller eyes than Emmentaler, and a stronger flavor.

Both kinds of cheese are used in fondue, which is sometimes called the national dish of Switzerland. The name means "melted," and fondue is made by melting grated cheese and adding Swiss wine and seasonings. After the fondue is brought to the table, it must be kept hot over a small flame.

In eating fondue, each person sitting around the table has a long-handled fork and a plate of crusty bread cut into small pieces. He spears a piece of bread with his fork, dips it into the bubbling cheese, and eats it while it is still hot.

The Swiss say that a man who drops the bread from his fork into the melted cheese must buy a glass of wine for everyone at the table. A girl who loses her piece of bread must pay her forfeit by giving her neighbor a kiss.

Besides Gruyère and Emmentaler, Swiss cheese makers make many other varieties of cheese, some hard and some soft, some strong and some mildly flavored. Altogether, they turn out about forty

*A chocolate bar is wrapped in two air tight coverings, then in an outside wrapper*

thousand tons of cheese a year — about twice what the Swiss themselves consume. Switzerland is thus able to export half her cheese production, or about forty million pounds a year. Swiss cheese has a fine reputation all over the world, and brings high prices. Cheese is therefore one of the country's most important exports, and the only important one made entirely of raw materials produced in Switzerland.

Every year about thirty million quarts of rich Swiss milk are delivered to chocolate-making factories. These factories also use sugar made from beets grown on Swiss farms. But they must import the expensive cocoa beans they use.

A Swiss chocolate factory is spotlessly clean, and full of delicious smells. Men in white uniforms tend the shiny machines that mix the ingredients of the candy. Experts prepare the nuts, fruits, and other fillings that are used. Girls in white uniforms decorate the bite-sized chocolates and the fancy shapes made for holidays — chocolate eggs and rabbits for Easter, chocolate stars and other ornaments for Christmas.

Big machines wrap every chocolate bar in two airtight coverings, and finally in a gaily printed outer wrapping.

One hundred hours of careful work go into the making of every piece of Swiss chocolate. The result is a smooth, rich candy as famous all over the world as Swiss cheese is.

Only about one-quarter of the chocolate is exported. The Swiss eat the rest themselves. They eat more chocolate than any other people in the world — about twice as much as Americans do, for example. They consume an average of over twelve pounds of candy a year for every man, woman, and child in the country.

# Also Made in Switzerland

SWITZERLAND has long been one of the most industrialized nations in the world. Some of the many industries that today employ more than half her population are fairly new; some are very old.

For more than four hundred years Swiss weavers have been importing cotton and silk and weaving it into beautiful cloth. Swiss-woven cotton and silk are still among the finest in the world. Modern Swiss weavers make many of today's synthetic fabrics, too.

Almost three hundred years ago some of the world's first watch-makers were Swiss farmers working in their spare time during the long winters. Each man learned to make just one part of a watch — the center wheel of the mechanism, perhaps, or the shaft on which the tiny wheels turn. This practice gave him the chance to learn his job thoroughly, and to invent ways of doing it better and better.

The farmer-craftsmen taught their skills to their sons. The sons in turn handed the knowledge on. Certain families became known for their careful, accurate workmanship. Each family helped make Swiss watches the finest that could be bought.

Today Swiss watchmaking is big business. Craftsmen in bright modern factories now turn out almost forty-five million timepieces a year — everything from ordinary wristwatches to complicated marine chronometers.

A modern Swiss watchmaker knows how to make all the 160-odd parts in every watch. He has learned his craft by studying for at least four years at a government-supported watchmaking school. Perhaps he has also done advanced work at the Swiss Research Laboratory for Watchmaking.

The experts in that laboratory designed the world's first atomic

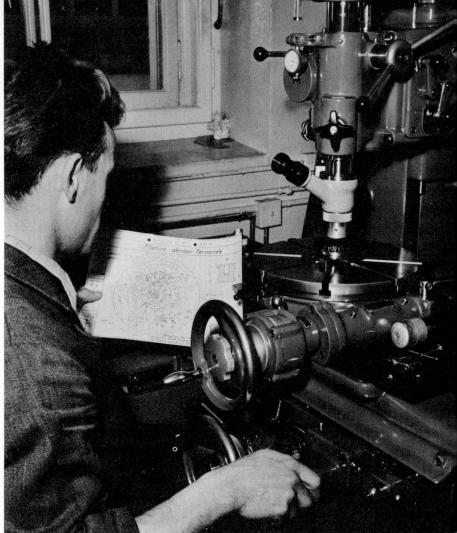

*Watchmaking demands precision machinery*

clock. They are responsible for most of the important improvements in modern timekeeping.

Today's Swiss watchmaker, like his ancestors, still concentrates on a single process, however. He may work in an assembly plant where completed watches are fitted into their cases and given the trade name by which they will be sold. He may make tiny, delicate watch springs.

23

*Watchmaking is a highly trained skill*

The workmen in a Swiss watch-spring factory once received a challenge from a group of German watchmakers. The Germans sent them a bit of watch spring so small that it could be seen only through a microscope.

"Can you match this?" the Germans asked.

The Swiss craftsmen didn't bother to make another tiny watch spring. They thought that would be too easy. Instead, they took the German bit of steel, almost as small as a speck of dust, and drilled a neat round hole in the middle of it. The Germans could scarcely believe their eyes when they looked at the metal through their microscope and saw what the Swiss had done.

24

Swiss watchmakers can transform a single pound of imported steel, which costs ten dollars, into sixty thousand dollars' worth of watch springs. Their skill earns them salaries that are among the highest paid to any craftsmen in the world.

In hundreds of small but efficient factories, Swiss craftsmen now transform many kinds of imported raw materials into products that compete successfully with goods made in lands richer in natural resources.

Swiss craftsmen make precision instruments and fine tools of many kinds. They make typewriters and cameras. They make machinery, including textile machines used in their important textile industry.

Swiss-made drugs and other chemical products are known to doctors, scientists, and farmers in every part of the world. The widely used insecticide called DDT first reached the public from a Swiss factory. Paul Mueller, the Swiss scientist who proved DDT's value as an insect-killer, received a Nobel prize for his work. More than a dozen other Swiss citizens have also won Nobel prizes.

JOE BOOG

*Important Swiss products are textiles*

Swiss-made marine engines now drive some of the world's biggest ocean-going ships. Swiss-made diesel engines pull trains across five continents.

Swiss industrial workers, most of them highly trained, will usually accept only highly skilled jobs. Foreign workers are imported to do most of the jobs that require little or no special skill. But even unskilled workers earn good wages in Switzerland. For this reason there are no slums in Swiss towns and cities. For this same reason, in addition to the existence of good working conditions, the members of Swiss labor unions almost never go on strike.

Not all of Switzerland's skilled craftsmen and equally skilled managers work inside their own country. Today many of them head the staffs of factories built outside of Switzerland, close to the sources of raw materials and close to the customers the factories supply.

These factories, owned and operated by Swiss, now carry the traditions of careful, precise Swiss workmanship into many other lands. And profits from these factories — profits earned by exporting Swiss skill and know-how — add to Switzerland's prosperity.

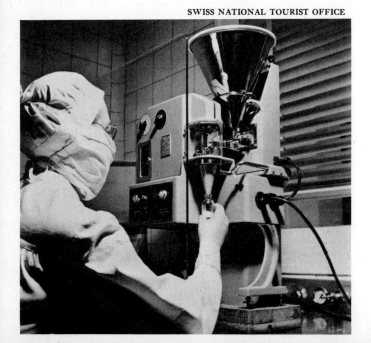

SWISS NATIONAL TOURIST OFFICE

*Drugs and chemicals are important Swiss products*

*Planes fly out to every quarter of the world from Zurich's great International Airport*

# Crossroads of the World

SWISS AIRPORTS are always busy. The planes of Switzerland's own airline fly regularly to more than forty countries. Foreign cargo and passenger planes from dozens of other nations land in Switzerland every day. A passenger arriving by jet at Zurich's big airport, for example, may be coming in from the north — and may leave from there for the south, the west, or the east. Switzerland is a crossroads of the world's air travel.

This little country has always been a crossroads of world traffic, in spite of her lack of a seacoast and seaports.

27

*The Rhine River roars over these falls on the border between Switzerland and Germany*

Switzerland, moreover, has only one river port, although rivers flow out from her Alpine glaciers in all directions. The Rhine flows northward through Germany and the Netherlands, and empties into the North Sea. The Ticino flows southward into Italy to join the Po, on its way to the Adriatic. The Inn River flows eastward into Austria, to become a part of the Danube before it reaches the Black Sea. The Rhone flows eastward into France and on into the Mediterranean. But there is no connection between the northward-flowing Rhine and the southward-flowing Ticino. There is no connection between the eastward-flowing Inn and the westward-flowing Rhone.

Basel, on the Rhine, is the only Swiss city from which cargo can reach the ocean. Most of the shipments leaving Basel travel by barge to Rotterdam. There they can be transferred to oceangoing vessels. Switzerland has had its own oceangoing merchant fleet since World War II.

Centuries before today's air age the traffic that made Switzerland a crossroads of the world was that which moved by land through the Alpine passes. Seventeen of these passes cross the Alps from north to south; three cross from east to west. Each pass was originally nothing more than a narrow mule track or footpath — a trail through the mountains, picked out by men who needed to make their way from one side of the Alpine range to the other.

Most of the Alpine passes reach altitudes of more than a mile and

*The Rhine River connects the harbor of Basel with the sea*

a half above sea level, and are buried beneath snow for many months of the year. Early travelers never found a really easy route among the towering peaks. They ran great risks, especially during the winter. Almost a thousand years ago, one man, a priest who came to be known as St. Bernard, took pity on them. He built a hut near the pass now called the Great St. Bernard, and stationed monks there to help lost wayfarers. The big dogs the monks trained to aid them in their lifesaving task are still called St. Bernards.

The first paved roads through the Alps are only about 150 years old, and the railroads through the passes are even younger. Even the

*A viaduct carries a train across a chasm below a castle built nine hundred years ago*

*This head of a Roman emperor, made of gold, was found at the little town of Avenches, where the Roman city of Aventicum stood two thousand years ago*

PHOTOPRESS, ZURICH

finest roads and railroad tracks may become impassable in winter, however. For this reason the Swiss have dug tunnels beneath some of the busiest passes.

The tunnel under St. Gotthard Pass, more than nine miles long, was built in the 1880's. Some two hundred men lost their lives during the work, which was one of the greatest engineering feats of the nineteenth century.

The tunnel under the Simplon Pass is even longer than that at St. Gotthard. When it was finished in 1906 it ran a record-breaking twelve miles underground, and at its deepest point burrowed more than a mile below the surface.

Over two thousand years ago, the armies of ancient Rome made use of the Alpine passes to conquer most of Europe, including the region that is now Switzerland. That region was then named Helvetia, because the Celtic people who lived there were known as Helvetii. In Roman days, Helvetia's capital was the big walled city of Aventicum, which had a population of two hundred thousand. Now the small Swiss town of Avenches stands on Aventicum's site.

31

Part of the ancient Roman wall still exists, and many relics of Roman days have been found buried in the land.

Roman soldiers and traders traveling northward over the passes brought the Roman civilization to Helvetia. Missionaries carrying the Christian religion throughout Europe used the passes, too. For hundreds of years those passes helped hold the vast Roman Empire together.

In about the year A.D. 450 the empire was destroyed by Germanic hordes from northern Europe, who forced their way south through the passes. Germans then settled in what is now eastern Switzerland. At the same time, French Burgundians seized and occupied western Switzerland.

From that time on, many powers struggled for control of the valuable passes. In A.D. 800, for example, the great Charlemagne held the St. Gotthard Pass and thus controlled a vast domain known for several centuries as the Holy Roman Empire.

Almost seven hundred years ago one of the struggles for the control of that same pass gave birth to the republic of Switzerland.

*The magnificent library of the St. Gall monastery holds treasures that date back to the time of Charlemagne, whose vast empire included present-day Switzerland*

# A Nation Is Born

IN THE YEAR 1291 there were three small forest cantons, or states of the Holy Roman Empire, near the St. Gotthard Pass. Their names were Uri, Unterwalden, and Schwyz. Their German inhabitants were farmers, hunters, and woodcutters.

For the most part, the emperor permitted Austrian and Burgundian noblemen to govern the states in his empire. Each nobleman owned the people who lived in his state, and treated them as serfs, or slaves. But the emperor kept the little cantons of Uri, Unterwalden, and Schwyz under his personal authority, and treated their inhabitants as free men, with the right to live their own lives in their own way. In return for their liberty, the men of these three cantons served as the emperor's guardians for the vital St. Gotthard Pass.

The day arrived when the Austrian noblemen wanted to control that pass themselves, as a first step toward taking over the whole empire. They threatened to seize the three cantons. With seizure, the men of the cantons knew they would lose their freedom under Austrian rule. And because they also knew that their emperor was too weak to defeat the threatening nobles, they determined to fight the Austrians alone.

On August 1, 1291, the three cantons formed a league and signed a pact of mutual protection and defense. That date is now honored as the birthday of Switzerland — the beginning of the Swiss nation. Switzerland takes its name from the little canton of Schwyz.

Not long after the pact was signed, the new league of three cantons met and defeated in open battle the forces of the Austrians. It was an important victory for the Switzers, as they came to be called.

Wonderful tales of Swiss courage and independence began to be

33

*Today a modern highway, as well as a railroad, threads its way through the narrow St. Gotthard Pass*

told in the Alpine villages near the St. Gotthard Pass. One was the story of William Tell, who probably never really existed, but who is the most popular folk hero of Switzerland.

A cruel Austrian official, so the legend goes, commanded William Tell, who had defied him, to shoot an apple from his son's head. The official hoped young Tell would be killed. But William Tell was such a skillful bowman, according to the story, that he split the apple in two without harming a hair of the boy's head. Afterward Tell waited for his enemy on a lonely mountain path, and assassinated him.

Gradually, neighboring cantons decided that they too wanted to escape Austrian control and win freedom. By 1353, five of them had joined the league, or Confederation, as it was later called. Once inside the Confederation, they too refused to accept any authority except that of the emperor himself.

*A monument to Switzerland's legendary hero, William Tell*

*Zurich is proud of its guild halls, built centuries ago by the powerful guilds of craftsmen that once ruled the city*

During the next two centuries the Confederation grew even larger. Most of the new member cantons joined by their own choice. A few were conquered by the Confederation and held as the joint possession of the other cantons.

Membership in the league did not change a canton's customs or ways of life; each clung to its own traditions. In some cantons the people themselves formed the government, voting on important matters at open-air meetings. In others, authority was in the hands of powerful guilds of traders and craftsmen, or aristocratic families. But in time of danger the cantons lived up to their confederation's motto: "All for one and one for all."

In 1476, Charles the Bold of Burgundy threatened to seize the cantons, but their united forces defeated him. In 1499 they fought the emperor himself, because he tried to force them to pay a new tax. The cantons' victory over the emperor's army made them independent of him.

36

The Switzers had become famous as fighters. Carrying eighteen-foot-long pikes, they moved forward in battle in a solid column, pikes thrust outward. A Swiss battle formation looked like a huge, menacing porcupine. The Swiss call that time in their history the "heroic period." During this period the most ambitious rulers of Europe sought Swiss friendship, and aid against their enemies. The Swiss fought as allies of the Duke of Milan, and they fought as allies of the Duke's French enemies.

They met their first serious defeat in 1515. That date marks the end of their "heroic period." From then on, the Confederation refused to take part in the quarrels of other European powers. This decision was Switzerland's first step toward her present-day neutrality.

*Today the only Swiss who wear foreign uniforms are the young Catholics chosen to serve as the guard of the Pope, at the Vatican in Rome. Here three of them help each other dress in their brilliant red-and-yellow uniforms, designed by Michelangelo over four hundred years ago*

*Bishop Zwingli preached against the power of the Pope and won many followers to his Protestant movement*

For several centuries, however, other European powers went on hiring Swiss soldiers to help them fight their battles. Fighting for pay was one way the Swiss helped support themselves, at a time when countries with big navies — Spain, for example, and France and England — were finding wealth in their New World colonies.

Since the cantons did not always live at peace with one another, Swiss soldiers fought on their own territory, too. Sometimes a war broke out because certain cantons wanted to control others; sometimes the cantons quarreled for religious reasons.

38

Switzerland's religious wars began at the time of the Reformation, when the Protestants were breaking away from the Catholic Church. Some cantons remained Catholic; others did not. In the canton of Zurich, for example, a peasant-born bishop, Ulrich Zwingli, preached against the power of the Pope and won many followers for his Protestant movement. Zurich was one of the cantons that became officially Protestant, and thus was opposed to the cantons governed by Catholics.

Catholic and Protestant cantons fought one another many times before religious freedom was finally established in Switzerland. Today more than half the country's population is Protestant. About four out of every ten Swiss are Catholic. The remainder of the population — those who are neither Catholic nor Protestant — are Jews or nonbelievers. All Swiss are free to worship, or not to worship, as they wish.

The American War for Independence (1775-1781) won warm friends among the freedom-loving Swiss. They also sympathized with the French Revolution. But when Napoleon Bonaparte made himself the new ruler of France and set out to conquer a vast empire, he decided that he must first control Europe's crossroads — Switzerland and her Alpine passes.

The Swiss could not withstand Napoleon's huge army. In 1798 they found themselves overrun by a foreign power for the first time in centuries. Napoleon forced the Swiss to pay taxes to him. He enrolled Swiss citizens in his army. Some Swiss welcomed his revolutionary ideas. People in cantons that had been ruled by powerful aristocrats and guilds or by other cantons felt freer under Napoleon than they had before. But the Swiss Confederation had lost its independence; it had become a part of France.

Finally the combined power of other European leaders defeated Napoleon, and terms of peace were agreed on in a treaty drawn up at Vienna.

The powers that signed the treaty knew how useful the Alpine passes had been to Napoleon, and they wished to guard against those passes ever falling again into the hands of a power ambitious to conquer the world. Accordingly, the Treaty of Vienna declared that Switzerland should remain neutral for all time.

This decision meant that Switzerland could not ally herself with any other nation and thus give that nation the right to send armies through her passes. Switzerland's neutrality, in other words, was meant to be a safeguard for European peace.

The Swiss had already proved that they could remain neutral while their neighbors were at war. They willingly gave their pledge to remain neutral in the future — to keep the Alpine passes open to peaceful traffic at all times, and never to permit their use by an army bent on conquest.

The other European powers, in their turn, promised to respect Switzerland's neutrality — never to seek her as an ally and never to attack her as an enemy.

During the century and a half since the Treaty of Vienna was signed, most of its agreements have been broken at one time or another. But Switzerland's neutrality has endured to this day. That neutrality has played an important role in Europe's history. It has also helped Switzerland, small as she is and poor in natural resources, to develop into a prosperous modern nation.

# Democracy, Swiss Style

ASK A SWISS the name of his country's President, and he will probably not be able to tell you, although he will probably know the names of other important world leaders, and know a good deal about them, too.

Some 450 newspapers and more than 2,500 magazines and other journals keep the Swiss well informed on world affairs, and conditions in Switzerland as well. But their President is not well known because he is not a man who has been chosen by the people to serve as their leader.

The President is simply one of the seven men who make up a body called the Federal Council. This council might be compared to the Cabinet of an American President or a British Prime Minister.

*For the size of its population, Switzerland has more newspapers than any other country*

*The two houses, or councils, of the Swiss Federal Assembly meet in these buildings in Bern*

Each council member heads a government department. One heads the Department of the Interior, for example; another heads the Political Department and is in charge of foreign affairs. Every year one member of the council serves as its president, and as President of the Confederation of Switzerland.

The President receives a higher salary than other council members, but does not earn enough to pay for servants and a big car. He continues to live in his own home, usually a small apartment.

He greets foreign rulers who visit Switzerland, and receives the ambassadors sent to his country. He may represent Switzerland at an international meeting of chiefs of state. But he continues to handle

42

*The Council of States meets in this chamber*

the work of his department, and at the end of a year his term of office as President is over — though he may be named President again two or more years later.

Switzerland's national government is stronger than the loose organization that once bound the cantons together for protection. When it was remodeled in 1848 it was given a form copied partly after the government of the United States.

Switzerland's Federal Assembly, for example, is similar in some ways to the United States Congress. It consists of two houses, one called the Council of States, the other the National Council.

The Council of States, like the United States Senate, consists of

43

two members from each state, or canton. But, unlike an American state, each canton decides on the method for selecting its own Council members. It may choose them by popular election. It may let its own cantonal Assembly elect them.

Each canton also decides on the number of years its Council members will serve. Some have four-year terms, others one-year. Each canton also pays its own members.

The Assembly's other house, the National Council — like the United States House of Representatives — consists of members that have been elected according to population. It has one member for about every 24,000 people, or about 200 members altogether.

Bern, the biggest canton, is represented by over thirty men. Uri, one of the smallest cantons, by only one. The members are chosen in such a way that they also represent the nation's half-dozen or so political parties. They are paid by the national treasury.

In order to pass a new law, both councils of the Assembly must first approve it. Then they must offer it for the people's approval. If no widespread objection is made, the law automatically goes into effect at the end of ninety days. But if many people dislike the law, they take matters into their own hands. They draw up a petition asking that the law be put to a vote. If there are at least thirty thousand signatures on the petition, the councils must put the law to a vote of the whole population.

The people have another way of taking part directly in lawmaking, too. Citizens who want to add an amendment to the constitution, for example, submit their amendment to the councils, along with a petition signed by at least fifty thousand citizens. Then the government must put the amendment to a public vote.

Both councils of Switzerland's Federal Assembly meet in Bern. The seven-man Federal Council (which is appointed by the As-

*A bear is the symbol of Bern, and this bear pit is one of the most popular places in the city*

sembly) also meets in Bern. But the Swiss do not think of this city as their capital in the same way that Americans think of Washington as their federal city. Switzerland's two federal courts, for example, sit in two other cities, one in Lausanne, the other in Lucerne.

The first court, the Federal Court of Justice at Lausanne, tries criminal cases and settles various disputes — between two cantons, for example, or between a canton and the Confederation. It can decide whether or not a law passed by a canton is constitutional. It does not decide on the constitutionality of federal laws. The Swiss people themselves are the final authority on those laws.

The other federal court is the Federal Insurance Tribunal, at Lucerne. It settles only cases that have to do with insurance for sickness, accident, and so on. There are a good many such cases, because all Swiss workers have old-age insurance, along with at least one life

45

insurance policy, and perhaps policies of several other kinds as well. Insurance is a popular form of saving among the thrifty Swiss. Their insurance companies have such an excellent reputation that foreigners often insure themselves in Switzerland, or with one of the many foreign branches of Swiss companies.

The federal government is responsible for the country's foreign policy and defense — and, incidentally, for the foreign policy of its tiny neighbor, the principality of Liechtenstein.

The federal government runs Switzerland's postal, telephone, and telegraph services, and her railroads. It controls the national economy. It supports a museum which displays the folk art and ancient costumes of all the cantons, along with relics of the early time when prehistoric men built houses on stilts in many of Switzerland's numerous lakes.

*Government-owned buses deliver passengers and mail to remote mountain villages*

*The Swiss National Museum in Zurich*

SWISS NATIONAL TOURIST OFFICE

The federal government also supports the Federal Institute of Technology, a famous university that attracts students from all over the world.

Switzerland's six other universities, along with its schools, most of its roads, and almost everything else in the country, are controlled by the cantons. Each canton is governed by its own Assembly, and has its own courts and its own police force.

47

# Nobody Speaks Swiss

NOBODY speaks "Swiss." There is no Swiss language.

Instead, the people of each canton speak the language their ancestors used when they first joined the Swiss Confederation.

Those who live in the northeastern and central cantons — almost three-quarters of the Swiss population — speak German. Their schools are taught in German. Their books and newspapers are printed in German. When they talk among themselves they use a dialect called Schwyzerdütsch, or Swiss-German, which a visitor from Germany or Austria might not understand, but their written language is the same German spoken in those two countries. German-speaking Swiss call their own country Schweiz.

*One message in four languages: this sign at the St. Gotthard Pass tells travelers that the pass is now open, and gives directions to those wishing to go through it by train, after loading their autos on railroad flatcars*

*A house in the canton of Grisons, where people speak Switzerland's "fourth" language, Romansh*

In three western cantons along the border of France — the Vaud, Neuchâtel, and Geneva — people speak French. They insist that their language is a better and purer French than the one spoken in France. They call their country by its French name, Suisse.

In the southern canton of Ticino, on the Italian border, people speak Italian. In their language the name of their country is Svizzera.

All three of these languages are "official" languages of Switzerland. For example, when a new federal law is passed, it must be printed in all three — German, French, and Italian.

A fourth language is spoken in Switzerland, too, in parts of the big eastern canton of Grisons. It is called Romansh. Like French and Italian, it comes from the Latin language of the ancient Romans, but it is much closer to Latin than either of those two tongues. In Romansh the name of Switzerland is Svizra.

Federal laws do not have to be printed in Romansh, but the people who speak this strange tongue have the same rights all Swiss have: to use their own language in their schools, and for their newspapers, their street signs, and all other purposes.

Swiss children often learn at least one foreign language, such as English or Spanish, but they must all know at least two of the languages of their own country. Beginning in the sixth grade, German-speaking children are taught French. French-speaking and Italian-speaking children begin to study German at the same time. Romansh-speaking children learn one of the country's three official languages.

# A Little World

ALMOST AS SOON as they arrive, visitors notice that no two cantons in Switzerland are alike. Visitors usually agree with the traveler who said long ago that Switzerland was "not a little country, but a little world."

Two cantons may be as different as two countries — chiefly, of course, because each canton was once a small separate nation or state with its own background and way of life.

The differences show, for example, in the kinds of houses people live in. Farmers in the Ticino have solid stone houses roofed with flat stones. The people in this canton have been famous stonemasons for centuries, and there are many quarries in their rocky mountains.

*Some Swiss farmhouses are built of stone*

*Some farmhouses are built of wood*

The wooden cottages in Appenzell, with their wide, overhanging roofs and carved window boxes, show their owners' skill at woodworking and at making good use of their forests.

Village houses in the canton of Zurich have white-painted plaster walls crisscrossed with dark timbers. They look like the homes seen in many villages of neighboring Germany. The handsome homes in the canton's big city, Zurich, show the wealth of this large center of trade and industry.

*Some farmhouses are built of plaster and timbers*

*Housefronts in Stein-am-Rhein are decorated with huge painted figures and scenes. The sign of the golden sun on this one shows that it is now an inn — the Sun Hotel*

*The medieval castle and village of Regensburg, in the canton of Zurich*

Many houses in Schaffhausen and the nearby town of Stein-am-Rhein are being preserved as historical monuments, as are some of the ancient castles that stand along Switzerland's lakes and riverbanks. These houses are particularly interesting because of the big figures and scenes painted on their fronts in vivid colors.

55

*A solemn St. Nicklaus asks children if they have been good during the past year. The black shape behind him is his "Schmutzli"*

Each canton has its own festivals and holidays. December 6, for example, is the day of St. Nicklaus all over Switzerland, but each canton celebrates it in its own way. In some places a white-robed St. Nicklaus — a kind of solemn Santa Claus — goes from house to house with his "Schmutzli." The Schmutzli, an ugly figure dressed in

*The boys of Zurich march in a parade to honor St. Nicklaus*

black and carrying a whip, threatens to carry off naughty children. St. Nicklaus always persuades him that none of them really deserves such severe punishment. In other places the figure of St. Nicklaus leads a parade and tosses presents to small boys and girls.

*Every December 10, the Genevese dress in medieval costume to celebrate an ancient victory*

Geneva, which became the twenty-second and last canton to join the Swiss Confederation, in 1815, celebrates the memory of some of its own famous citizens. One of those men was the preacher John Calvin, who made Geneva a world center of the Reformation movement in the sixteenth century. Another was Jean Jacques Rousseau, whose ideas about the rights of man inspired both the American and French revolutionists.

December 10 is an important holiday in Geneva, because on December 10, 1602, the people of the city defeated an attack by the powerful Duke of Savoy. Now, every year on that day, hundreds of Genevese dress in medieval costumes and act out their ancestors' victory celebration. They parade through the narrow streets of the old part of the city, carrying torches, and then join in hymns of thanksgiving around a huge bonfire.

Every March the Genevese wait for a certain century-old chestnut tree to put forth its first green leaf. A city official watches for the leaf, and writes the date in the city records. Newspapers report the leaf's unfolding, too. In Geneva its coming means that spring has arrived — even if Mont Blanc, in the distance, is still covered with snow far down its slopes.

The people of Zurich welcome spring every year with two great costume parades, one for children, one for grown-ups. A cart pulled through the streets by the children holds a huge snowman, made of cotton wool. He is the *Böögg*, the spirit of winter. At the end of the parade the *Böögg* is placed high on a pole in the center of the city. Later, after the grown-ups have paraded, everybody gathers to watch the burning of the *Böögg*.

*The people of Zurich carry a big cotton snowman, called the* Böögg, *to his death on a huge bonfire. The burning of the* Böögg *heralds the coming of spring*

# The Ballot and the Raised Hand

THE WAY PEOPLE vote, and the number of times they vote, also change from canton to canton. In some cantons, councils of elected officials decide many questions without putting them to a public vote. In others the citizens themselves must vote on almost every decision that must be made. They may even vote on the teachers they want in their public schools. A Swiss citizen may be called upon to vote as often as once a month, year in and year out.

In Zurich, people receive their ballots by mail. A voter may do one of three things with his ballot. He may mark his vote on it, and deliver it to the voting place by a certain day. He must do this in order to make his vote count.

Or he may mail his ballot to the authorities within a certain period of time. In this case his vote will not be counted, but he will avoid the payment of a penalty.

SWISS NATIONAL TOURIST OFFICE

*Voters put on traditional costumes to march to an open-air meeting where they will hold elections*

*Citizens of Glarus gather in the Ring to vote. Boys stand close to the central stage, to learn the duties of citizenship*

If he neither delivers his ballot nor mails it in, a police officer comes to his house to collect it. Then the citizen must pay a penalty — a small fee to cover the cost of collection.

In the five smallest cantons, men still vote in open-air meetings. The form of democracy they practice is one of the oldest in the world.

One of these cantons is Glarus, a narrow valley set among high mountains. Here citizens meet, to hold an election or vote on a new law, in what they call the Ring. It is an open space surrounded by rows of wooden seats, with a raised stage at its center. The young boys of the canton are gathered around the stage so that they may hear what goes on and learn the duties of citizenship. Each boy will

61

*The men of Appenzell carry their swords on the day of their open-air election meeting*

assume those duties when he is twenty. No women are present. Only three cantons give women the right to vote.

Officials in colorful uniforms, who march into the Ring to the sound of music, speak on the questions to be decided. The citizens discuss them, too. Then they cast their votes by raising their hands. They know that in other cantons, as in many other countries, men vote by secret ballot, but they prefer their own method. They say it gives them the chance to prove that they are not afraid to express their opinions in public. This kind of courage, they believe, earns men the right to freedom.

The men of Glarus have often proved that they have the courage to vote in favor of new ideas. In 1864 this canton, which has many factories, passed Europe's first law for the protection of workers.

In the canton of Appenzell the men wear swords to their open-air meetings. They are following a custom of their ancestors, who wore swords to prove that they could defend themselves. Long ago, in Appenzell, only men who were able to defend themselves were permitted to vote.

62

# The Swiss Citizen

A Swiss USUALLY speaks of himself as a Swiss only when he is in a foreign country. At home he is more likely to say, "I'm from the canton of Geneva," or "I'm from the Vaud." He sounds rather like an American who introduces himself by saying, "I'm a Californian," or "I'm from Texas."

A Swiss may not speak so often of his commune — that is, the village or town from which his family comes. In many ways, however, he feels closer to his commune than to his canton.

Long ago, a commune might be cut off from the rest of the world for much of the year, perhaps by snow, perhaps by flooding streams. Then each town or village had to handle its own affairs and solve its own problems. Today it still does, to a large extent.

There are 3,100 communes in Switzerland. They are the basic units that make up the Swiss democracy. In Switzerland, every commune is responsible for the well-being of its own citizens. A

*A snowbound commune, or village*

citizen may leave his commune as a young man, and spend most of his life in another town — even in another country. But if that citizen is ever in need — if he is sick or destitute — he can return to his commune and be cared for.

Of course, every citizen of a commune is automatically a citizen of his canton too, and therefore of Switzerland. But the right of citizenship can come only from the commune — not from the canton or the federal government.

A foreigner who settles in Switzerland and wishes to become a citizen must apply to the commune where he lives. In most cases he must wait several years and perhaps pay a large fee before the citizenship is granted. In the meantime, however, he will probably be allowed to vote on certain questions that affect all the commune's residents, citizens and noncitizens alike.

A man who leaves his commune always takes with him the diploma, or certificate, that proves his citizenship. He may use it to help establish his Swiss citizenship, in the commune he moves to. But in any case he keeps his original commune citizenship, and hands it on to his sons and grandsons. Thus they too are citizens of his commune, even though they may never live in it. By fulfilling certain requirements, they may transfer their citizenship to the commune where they actually live. Many prefer not to.

No one can really understand Switzerland who does not understand that every Swiss is firstly a citizen of his commune, secondly a citizen of his canton, and only thirdly a citizen of Switzerland. The citizens of Switzerland's communes, however, have built a strong and prosperous nation because they have learned how to unite on certain issues and face the outside world as a solid confederation.

One of the things on which they stand united is Switzerland's neutrality.

# What Neutrality Means

EVERY SWISS citizen knows that neutrality often brings duties and burdens that people in non-neutral countries do not have to carry.

Take the case of a Swiss ambassador, for example. Let's say that his name is Schmid and that he serves as ambassador to a country called X. And let's say that country X goes to war against country Y.

When war is declared, Y's ambassador to X is called home. Before he leaves, he visits Schmid to ask his help. He knows that Schmid will remain at his post in X because neutral Switzerland will not go to war. Therefore Y's ambassador asks Schmid to take over the work he must leave behind.

He asks Schmid to look after the safety of all the citizens of Y who remain in X, or who have business there. He also asks him to do everything possible for soldiers or civilians of Y who may be captured during the war and imprisoned by their enemies.

If other nations also declare war on X and call their ambassadors home, these men usually leave their affairs in Schmid's hands, too. During World War II, Switzerland's diplomats, at their various posts, were handling the affairs of some forty nations.

Neutrality also means that when a war occurs somewhere in the world, Switzerland is likely to be crowded with refugees from the warring nations. The neutral Swiss help the refugees in any way they can, supplying them with food, clothes, shelter, and protection from their enemies.

Sometimes, when the warring nations include those from which Switzerland normally imports most of her foodstuffs, the Swiss have very little food even for themselves. In World War II, for example, Switzerland was completely surrounded by German-controlled ter-

65

*During and after World War II, Switzerland cared for thousands of home-less refugee children. These lived in the first Pestalozzi Children's Village, named after a famous nineteenth-century Swiss educator. Today there are many of these Children's Villages*

ritory. Nazi Germany herself was unwilling to export food to Switzerland because her own supplies were growing scarce. Germany's enemies, the Allied nations including the United States, could not make any deliveries of food to Switzerland through German-controlled country.

Switzerland was sheltering a hundred thousand refugees from France, Austria, Poland, and other countries seized by Germany. Among the refugees, for a time, were a whole French army corps and an entire division of Polish soldiers. In addition, many Allied airmen, shot down over enemy territory, had made their way into Switzerland.

To feed these refugees and themselves, the Swiss planted potatoes in every possible place. They plowed up the green lawns and flower beds of city parks, and replaced them with potato fields. They dug up the narrow strips of grass between sidewalks and streets, and planted potatoes there too. Homeowners pulled up prize-winning roses to make room for potatoes. Apartment-dwellers and cottage-dwellers grew potatoes in window boxes. Nobody starved in Switzerland during the long years of the war, but most people did become rather tired of potatoes.

Neutrality has definite benefits for Switzerland, however. It brings millions of dollars from all over the world into Swiss banks.

In a country that is at war, prices usually go up, and the rise reduces the value of that country's currency. If the price of bread is raised from twenty cents to forty cents a loaf, for example, every dollar spent for bread buys only half as much as it did in peacetime. When this sort of rise happens, businessmen say that the country's currency is inflated.

Because Switzerland does not go to war, her currency is not inflated. A franc, the Swiss unit of money, remains at about the same value year after year. Therefore a citizen of country X, who changes his money into Swiss francs and leaves it in a Swiss bank, feels quite sure that its value will not be reduced even if the currency of X becomes inflated.

Swiss bankers protect in many ways the people who bank with them. An account in a Swiss bank is given a number, which is known only to the owner of the money and to the bank. The name for which the number stands remains a secret between the banker and its owner.

# Geneva: International City

TALL FLAGSTAFFS line one of the beautiful bridges over the Rhone River, which flows through Geneva. The twenty-two different banners that fly from them are the flags of Switzerland's twenty-two cantons.

Those flags are a symbol that the Swiss cantons, once separate states often quarreling among themselves, now live in peaceful unity in spite of their differences of language, belief, and custom.

The people of Switzerland are hopeful that someday all the nations of Europe — perhaps all the nations of the world — will be able to live in peaceful unity in spite of their differences. The Swiss believe that the unity of their own nation, where every man respects the right of his neighbor to be different from himself, could serve as a useful model for a larger unity of nations.

They also believe that the neutrality of their nation is one step toward that peaceful goal. A Swiss citizen puts it this way: "We have pledged never to make war on another nation. We mean to keep our pledge. If every country made and kept the same pledge, war would be outlawed."

International organizations — people of many lands working together for a common good — are, the Swiss believe, another step toward world peace. They welcome the many such organizations that make their headquarters in Switzerland, most of them in Geneva.

One of the oldest and most important of these organizations is the International Red Cross. It was founded by a Swiss citizen in 1863, and has always received a great deal of Swiss support. It helped make Geneva what it is today — a truly international city.

Today's Red Cross societies, in nearly a hundred nations, have

*Red Cross relief parcels filled dozens of Swiss warehouses during World War II*

INTERNATIONAL COMMITTEE OF THE RED CROSS

millions of members who are trained and ready to assist victims of both war and disaster. They are organized into a league that has its headquarters in Geneva.

A separate organization, the small group of Swiss forming the International Committee of the Red Cross — usually called the ICRC — works closely with the league. The ICRC now has some twenty-five members, and can call on hundreds of other Swiss citizens for help in time of emergency. Almost every time fighting breaks out anywhere in the world, ICRC delegates go immediately to the scene of the conflict. Often they work there with Swiss diplomats and with Swiss businessmen who automatically offer their aid in time of trouble — or they may have to work alone.

*The Palace of Nations in Geneva*

They inspect prison camps, to make sure the prisoners are being treated decently. They distribute Red Cross relief parcels. They arrange truces to permit the exchange of prisoners. They are always unarmed and often in great danger. Many Swiss have lost their lives on these missions.

During World War II the ICRC did a great deal of important work. One of its activities was forming an agency for keeping war prisoners in touch with their families. Early in the war, a few people working in a single room could handle the queries that came in. Later the agency's staff numbered more than twenty-five hundred, and was using acres of office space in Geneva and twenty-seven other Swiss cities. Its file of prisoners contained 36 million cards. Twenty years after the war was over, the ICRC was still working with a huge file of persons lost or missing during that conflict. By then, of course, it was doing work of many other kinds, too.

The ICRC helps carry out the agreements known as the Geneva Convention — international agreements guaranteeing humane treatment of war victims. The Convention was signed in Geneva. It proved, for the first time, that nations could cooperate for the good of mankind even during a war. It paved the way for the League of Nations, formed after World War I, and for the United Nations, formed after World War II.

One of the most important buildings in Geneva today is the Palace of Nations. It was built originally as headquarters for the League of Nations. Now it is the European office of the United Nations.

Near the Palace of Nations are the headquarters of WHO and ILO, the United Nation's World Health and International Labor organizations. Switzerland belongs to both these organizations, to UNESCO (United Nations Educational, Scientific and Cultural Organization), and to international groups that encourage the free trade among nations which she has always believed in. Her neutrality keeps her out of the United Nations itself, because that organization's charter permits sending military forces into certain areas — and Switzerland can take no part in any activity of that kind.

The International Council of Churches has its headquarters in Geneva. So do many other religious, educational, and scientific groups whose members represent the nations of the world. Their names fill a whole directory published for the thousands of foreigners who come each year to this international city to work with the various groups or to attend their meetings and conferences.

# Citizen Soldiers

ALTHOUGH the Swiss know they will never attack any other nation, they cannot be certain they will always be safe from attack. They are prepared to defend themselves against any enemy who might attempt to cross their borders.

Hidden fortifications protect their Alpine passes. Tunnels through these passes are mined, and could be blown up at a moment's notice. Large supplies of food and equipment are stored in great vaults hol-

SWISS NATIONAL TOURIST OFFICE

*A Swiss Army ski unit trains in the high Alps*

lowed out of the mountains. And six hundred thousand men, expertly trained, uniformed and equipped — about one out of every ten persons in Switzerland — can report to their units, ready for active duty, within a few hours.

Switzerland has no regular army. The only Swiss who remain permanently in uniform are the few hundred men who serve as instructors in military training schools. None has the rank of general. When the country faces danger, Switzerland's Federal Assembly elects a general to lead her nation's forces. He resigns his post as soon as the danger is past.

Every healthy Swiss man is called up for military training when he is nineteen years old. He is excused only if he is physically unfit, and in that case he must contribute money to the government in the form of a tax.

His first period of training lasts about four months. From then on he trains with his unit for a brief period each year until he is forty-eight years old. He may be called up for further training or for active duty until he is sixty.

The Swiss citizen keeps his uniform, his gun, and forty rounds of ammunition in his own home. His equipment must be clean and in good condition at all times. He may also keep the horse, bicycle, motorcycle, or jeep that he uses in his unit. The government pays half its cost, the citizen the other half. He may use his horse or vehicle for his own private purposes, but it must always be ready — like the citizen himself — for immediate active duty under military orders.

Switzerland does not seek or accept military aid from any other nation. Her military equipment, mostly made in Switzerland with Swiss precision, is among the best in the world.

The Swiss believe that their freedom from attack during two

*Swiss citizen-soldiers must keep their army uniform and equipment in perfect order at all times*

world wars was the result of their preparedness. The whole world knew, they say, that they would defend their freedom and their neutrality to the last man.

Five centuries ago an Italian statesman said the Swiss were "very free and very well armed." Most statesmen would say the same thing about the Swiss today.

# Welcome to Switzerland

MANY TRAVELERS say they would rather visit Switzerland than any other country. Foreigners enjoy visiting Switzerland partly because the Swiss welcome them so warmly. There is almost always someone at hand who can speak the visitor's language. There are always many people ready to help him in every possible way. Whether the visitor is a millionaire, or a student traveling on a skimpy budget, the Swiss seem equally glad to see him and eager to make him feel at home.

*A village inn*

*Students at Swiss hotel-and-restaurant schools learn how to cook a meal*

They have not become the world's favorite hosts by accident, but have earned their position by long experience and careful training. Two big schools, one in Lausanne and one in Lucerne, teach the art of hotelkeeping — everything from bedmaking to sauce making, from how to press a jacket to how to serve a ten-course dinner.

In two other schools, at Geneva and Zurich, young men and women learn how to manage hotels and restaurants. They are taught how to choose the best meats and the most durable sheets and towels. In a big kitchen equipped with every variety of modern stove and cooking appliance they learn how to direct the preparation of hundreds of meals at once. In dining rooms open to the public they learn the duties of a waiter, and how to manage a staff of waiters. In classrooms they study languages and bookkeeping, tax laws and business law.

Those four schools are so famous that students from all over the world seek admission to them. A dozen possible jobs or more wait for every graduate.

Switzerland possesses a great natural resource in her mountains. The beauty and fascination of her Alps have helped bring her prosperity.

*The famous peak of the Matterhorn rises high above the village of Zermatt*

*Playing the game of curling*

During the nineteenth century one mountain village after another began to take in mountain climbers as guests. Inns were built, and then more inns.

Each year, mountain climbers set new goals for themselves. Until 1865, for example, the great Matterhorn had never been scaled. The summit of its jagged peak, nearly 15,000 feet above sea level, was believed to be beyond man's reach. But the Swiss guides and English sportsmen who tried it that year were successful. The news of their triumph went round the world.

Even when all the highest mountains had been climbed, men still found new challenges for their skill. They tried more difficult routes; they climbed under more difficult conditions. In 1962, almost a century after the Matterhorn was first climbed, two Swiss men made

78

the first winter ascent of its steep north face. They reached the top after a desperate race against teams from Germany and Austria.

In 1884 the world's longest toboggan run — a chute of ice twisting for three-quarters of a mile — was opened at the country's oldest and most fashionable resort, St. Moritz. Ice skating on frozen Swiss lakes was also becoming popular. So was curling, a game in which players send heavy stones along the ice toward a mark.

*These vacationers at an Alpine winter resort lunch out of doors and sunbathe in the snow*

*The Swiss Alpine Club builds shelters for climbers and skiers*

Then, in the twentieth century, skiing suddenly became the most popular of all Alpine sports. In the years since World War II, millions of foreign dollars have been spent at new Swiss ski schools, on Swiss ski tows and cable cars, and on Swiss-made ski equipment. And the Swiss themselves make as much use of their mountains as their foreign guests do. Every holiday morning the trains and highways leading out of their cities are crowded with climbers and skiers.

Today hundreds of Swiss work as mountain guides in the summer and as skiing instructors, or guides for skiing expeditions, in the winter. They too receive special training for their work. They must meet the high standards set by the Swiss Alpine Club, which has also built dozens of comfortable shelters in the mountains for the use of the guides and their parties.

A Swiss guide must know, first of all, everything about his mountains — their peaks and glaciers, their bare rock faces and forested slopes, their flowers and folklore. He must know the climbing and skiing trails best suited for amateurs and for experts. He must be able to protect a group of inexperienced newcomers from such dangers as avalanches, and the deep crevasses that sometimes open in the ice. He must be skilled at first aid and rescue work.

The Swiss Air Rescue Patrol, an organization of volunteers, is always ready to pick up an injured climber, or to parachute a doctor to a skier who has been hurt. The men of this unique patrol were once summoned across the Atlantic to help rescue plane-crash victims trapped deep in Arizona's Grand Canyon.

Most people, on seeing the Swiss Alps for the first time, stare at them in astonishment. They seem unable to believe the evidence of their own eyes.

*A mountain guide is highly trained to look after his party*

*Mountain climbing needs
sturdy shoes — and enough
time to admire the views*

The Swiss understand their amazement. They know that painters
and poets have almost always failed in their attempts to capture the
grandeur, the vastness, and the variety of these peaks. They know
that not even the finest photograph can portray the magnificence of
these mountains that rise up out of green valleys into the bright sun-
shine above the clouds.

"So you have come to see for yourself?" a Swiss innkeeper often
asks his guests. "Yes, it is the only way," he tells them.

He will make sure that his guests' stay will be comfortable. He
has already made them feel welcome. He has invited them to share
his homeland — the mountains that shaped his people's beginnings
and that have always shaped their lives.

# Index

# FIRST BOOKS
## Complete Check List

| Series No. | Quantity | TITLE Author | Listings | Grade Reading Level |
|---|---|---|---|---|
| 68 | | Atlas  C S Hammond & Co | A sl L | 3-4 |
| 22 | | Africa  Hughes | A sl L  CS | 4-7 |
| 140 | | Air  Knight | A sl L | 4 up |
| 1 | | Airplanes  Bendick | A sl L C CS | 3-6 |
| 76 | | American History  Commager | A sl L C CS | 4 up |
| 11 | | The American Revolution  Morris | A sl L C CS | 5 up |
| 158 | | Ancient Bible Lands  Robinson | New Publication | |
| 134 | | Ancient Egypt  Robinson | A  L | 4 up |
| 110 | | Ancient Greece  Robinson | A  L | 4 up |
| 150 | | Ancient Mesopotamia and Persia  Robinson | A  L | 4 up |
| 99 | | Ancient Rome  Robinson | A  L | 4 up |
| 73 | | The Antarctic  Icenhower | A  L C | 4-7 |
| 77 | | Archaeology  Kubie | A sl L C CS | 4 up |
| 135 | | Architecture  Moore | A sl L | 4 up |
| 104 | | Astronomy  Grey | A  L | 4 up |
| 107 | | Australia  Kaula | L | 4-7 |
| 5 | | Automobiles  Bendick | A sl L C CS | 3-5 |
| 44 | | The Ballet  Streatfeild | A sl L  CS | 4-7 |
| 148 | | Barbarian Invaders  Sobol | A | 5 up |
| 14 | | Baseball  Brewster | A sl L C CS | 3-5 |
| 94 | | Basketball  Schiffer | A sl L C | 4-8 |
| 4 | | Bees  Tibbets | A  L C CS | 3-6 |
| 98 | | Bells  Fletcher | L  CS | 2-4 |
| 18 | | Birds  Williamson | A  L C CS | 3-6 |
| 2 | | Boats  Gossett | A  L  CS | 2-4 |
| 101 | | Boys' Cooking  Beim | A sl L C CS | 4 up |
| 149 | | Brazil  Sheppard | A | 4 up |
| 43 | | Bridges  Peet | A  L C CS | 3-7 |
| 6 | | Bugs  Williamson | A sl L C CS H | 3-5 |
| 153 | | California Gold Rush  Havighurst | A  L | 4-7 |
| 65 | | Canada  C & M Lineaweaver | A  L C | 4-6 |
| 139 | | Cartoons for Kids  Fenner | | 2-5 |
| 111 | | Cats  Taber | A sl L C | 3-6 |
| 54 | | Caves  E Hamilton | A sl L C | 4-6 |
| 45 | | Chess  Leeming | A sl L C CS H | 5 up |
| 173 | | The China Clippers  Rich | New Publication | |
| 146 | | Christmas Joy  Wilson | A  L | 1-3 |
| 105 | | Civil War Land Battles  Dupuy | A sl L C | 5 up |
| 137 | | Civil War Naval Actions  Dupuy | A sl L | 5 up |
| 29 | | Codes and Ciphers  S & B Epstein | A sl L C CS H | 3-5 |
| 95 | | Color  Paschel | A  L C CS | 5 up |
| 157 | | Comunist China  Kinmond | New Publication | |
| 108 | | The Congo  McDonnell | L | 3-6 |
| 9 | | Congress  Coy | A sl L C  H | 5 up |
| 47 | | Conservation  F C Smith | A sl L C CS | 4-7 |
| 85 | | The Constitution  Morris | A sl L C CS | 5 up |
| 40 | | Cotton  Rogers | A  L C CS | 4-6 |
| 13 | | Cowboys  Brewster | A sl L C | 4 up |
| 10 | | Dogs  Taber | A  L C CS | 3-5 |
| 39 | | Dolls  H Hoke | A sl L C CS | 1-3 |
| 88 | | Drawing  Slobodkin | A sl L C | 6 up |
| 96 | | The Early Settlers  Rich | A sl L C | 4-6 |
| 81 | | The Earth  Sevrey | A  L C | 5 up |
| 42 | | Electricity  S & B Epstein | A sl L C CS | 4-8 |
| 83 | | England  Streatfeild | A  L C CS | 4-7 |
| 26 | | Eskimos  Brewster | A sl L C CS | 3-5 |
| 79 | | Fairy Tales  Abell | | 3 up |
| 25 | | Festivals  Reck | A  L C | 3-6 |
| 21 | | Firemen  Brewster | A  L | 3-5 |
| 69 | | Food  Scheib | A  L  CS | 3-5 |
| 87 | | Football  Schiffer | A sl L C | 3 up |
| 92 | | France  Gottlieb | A sl L C | 4-7 |
| 61 | | Gardening  Kirkus | A sl L C | 4-6 |
| 122 | | Ghana  Lobsenz | A sl L | 4-7 |
| 155 | | Glaciers  Marcus | A | 4 up |
| 60 | | Glass  S & B Epstein | A  L C CS | 3-5 |
| 48 | | Hawaii  S & B Epstein | A  L C CS | 4-6 |
| 62 | | Holidays  Burnett | A  L C | 3-5 |
| 8 | | Horses  McMeekin | A sl L C | 5 up |
| 129 | | How to Fix It  Bendick-Berk | A sl L | 3 up |
| 143 | | Human Senses  Liberty | A sl L | 4 up |
| 66 | | India  Hahn | L C CS | 4-7 |
| 103 | | The Indian Wars  Morris | A | 4 up |
| 15 | | Indians (American)  Brewster | A  L C CS | 2-6 |
| 41 | | Israel  Kubie | A sl L C CS | 4-7 |
| 89 | | Italy  S & B Epstein | A sl L C CS | 4-7 |
| 30 | | Japan  Mears | A  L C CS | 4-7 |
| 58 | | Jazz  Hughes | A  L C CS H | 7 up |
| 19 | | Jokes  Chrystie | A  L C CS | 3-6 |
| 130 | | Kings  Newton | L | 3-6 |
| 172 | | Language & How To Use It  Applegate | New Publication | |
| 159 | | Legendary Beings  Jacobson | New Publication | |
| 74 | | Letter Writing  Jacobson | A  L C CS | 4-6 |
| 160 | | Light  Harrison | New Publication | |
| 152 | | Machines  Buehr | A | 3-6 |
| 46 | | Magic  Stoddard | A sl L C CS | 3-5 |
| 75 | | Mammals  Williamson | A sl L C CS H | 4 up |
| 90 | | Maps and Globes  S & B Epstein | A sl L C CS | 4-6 |
| 125 | | Measurement  S & B Epstein | L | 4-6 |
| 102 | | Medieval Man  Sobol | A sl L | 4 up |
| 123 | | The Mediterranean  Gottlieb | A  L | 4-7 |
| 63 | | Mexico  S & B Epstein | A  L C  H | 4-7 |
| 35 | | Microbes  Lewis | A sl L C CS H | 4 up |
| 116 | | Mining  Markun | A  L | 3-6 |
| 51 | | Music  Norman | A sl L C CS | 3-6 |
| 128 | | Mythical Beasts  Jacobson | A  L | 3-5 |
| 67 | | Mythology  Elgin | A sl L  CS | 4 up |
| 113 | | National Monuments  Lobsenz | A  L | 3 up |
| 115 | | National Parks  Lobsenz | A  L | 3 up |
| 27 | | Negroes  Hughes | A sl L C CS | 4 up |
| 154 | | Netherlands  Cohn | A | 4 up |
| 12 | | New England  Rich | A  L  CS H | 4-6 |
| 119 | | New World Explorers  Rich | A  L | 4-6 |
| 131 | | New Zealand  Kaula | A | 4 up |
| 72 | | Norse Legends  Elgin | L | 4-6 |
| 16 | | Nurses  Elting | A sl L C CS | 3-5 |
| 133 | | Ocean  Epstein | A  L | 4 up |
| 109 | | The Oregon Trail  Havighurst | A  L C | 3-7 |
| 118 | | Paintings  Moore | A sl L C | 4 up |
| 151 | | Pakistan  Bothwell | A  L | 4 up |
| 84 | | The Panama Canal  Markun | A sl L C CS | 4 up |
| 50 | | Photography  J Hoke | A sl L C CS H | 5 up |
| 142 | | Physical Fitness  Walsh | A  L | 4 up |
| 97 | | Pioneers  Havighurst | | 4-8 |
| 38 | | Plants  Dickinson | A  C CS | 4 up |
| 37 | | Poetry  Peterson | A sl L C CS | 3-6 |
| 53 | | Prehistoric Animals  Dickinson | A sl L C CS | 4-7 |
| 28 | | Presidents  Coy | A  L  CS | 4-6 |
| 64 | | Printing  S & B Epstein | A sl L C CS H | 5 up |
| 114 | | Public Libraries  Graham | L | 2-4 |
| 24 | | Puppets  Jagendorf | A  L C | 3-5 |
| 49 | | Rhythms  Hughes | A sl L C CS | 2-4 |
| 55 | | Roads  Bothwell | A sl L C CS | 3-5 |
| 136 | | Sailing  M Lineaweaver | A  L C CS | 8 up |
| 31 | | Science Experiments  Wyler | A sl L C | 4-6 |

**ALL** are supplied in the Watts Guaranteed Library Binding

**ALL** are in large, clear type

**ALL** are fully illustrated—many with over 100 pictures, and in color

**ALL** checked and double-checked for accuracy, authority, and clarity of text

**ALL** 7¼ x 8¾ size

### KEY TO LISTINGS:

A  American Library Association, Booklist

sl  Booklist, Small Library Listing

L  Library Journal

C  H. W. Wilson Company, Children's Catalog

CS  Child Study Association of America, Books of the Year for Children

H  H. W. Wilson Company, High School Catalog

## What they say about
# FIRST BOOKS

"Their wide appeal, their broad coverage of varied subject areas, their wide range of significant and timely topics, and their attractive format and illustrations have made them valuable library materials."

MIRIAM PETERSON
*Chicago Board of Education*

"The format of each book has been superior and the books show that careful attention has been given to design, type, illustration, paper, and binding."

CAROLYN W. FIELD
*Philadelphia Public Library*

"I have long felt that the FIRST BOOKS developed (by Franklin Watts) were among the important creative contributions made by a publisher in recent decades."

PROF. HAROLD G. SHANE
*Indiana University*

"I really don't know how we ever ran our school libraries without the FIRST BOOKS!"

ELIZABETH HODGES
*Baltimore Board of Education*

"In covering a topic thoroughly, these books are like a junior encyclopedia, with an illustrated volume for each subject."

*Christian Science Monitor*

"Indeed an achievement! The high quality which has been maintained throughout the series is even more remarkable."

RUTH HILL VIGUERS
*The Horn Book*

"The FIRST BOOKS have made a real contribution in extending the horizons of their readers beyond the interests they knew they had."

JOSETTE FRANK
*Child Study Association of America*

Write for catalog. Address Dept. Sc

## FRANKLIN WATTS, INC. A Division
575 Lexington Avenue    New York 22, N. Y.    of Grolier Incorporated